THAT WINTER

That Winter

PAMELA GILLILAN

BLOODAXE BOOKS

ISBN: 1 85224 005 9

First published 1986 by
Bloodaxe Books Ltd,
P.O. Box 1SN,
Newcastle upon Tyne NE99 1SN.

This book is published with
the financial support of South West Arts

Bloodaxe Books Ltd acknowledges
the financial assistance of Northern Arts.

Typesetting by Bryan Williamson, Swinton, Berwickshire.

Printed in Great Britain by
Tyneside Free Press Workshop Ltd, Newcastle upon Tyne.

For Andrew, Lesley and Helen.

In memory of David.

Acknowledgements

Acknowledgements are due to the editors of the following publications in which some of these poems have appeared: *Anglo-Welsh Review*, *Giant Steps*, *The Green Book*, *Greenwich Literature Festival Anthology*, *The Honest Ulsterman*, *Iron*, *The Listener*, *New Poetry 8* (Hutchinson/Arts Council – P.E.N., 1982), *Outposts*, *Poetry Review*, *South West Review* and *Stand*.

'Coming to Terms', 'Daphne Morse', 'Four Years', 'Harvest' and 'Manchester' were broadcast on *Poetry Now* (BBC Radio 3). 'Come Away' won first prize in the 1979 Cheltenham Literature Festival/*Sunday Telegraph* poetry competition, and 'Pastoral' and 'Journey' won the 4th and 2nd prizes in the 1980 and 1981 Poetry Society national poetry competitions.

Contents

Manchester

A soiled light
Faltered through the window,
Died in the narrow room.
You lay like Eros on the shadowed bed.
I dared not look,
Wanted no sight to read your darkness
Nor any thought of time before or after
But a free-fall through the night.
These were the hours that could be
Our last together.

The hotel
Was half-destroyed by bombs,
Gritty with brickdust
And everywhere abraded by hard years;
Nap rubbed from the carpets,
Life eroded out of the old men waiters,
The wallpaper sad fawn and blackened gilt,
Chandeliers ready to fall
From their weight of dust.
We alone were young.

Two days we had.
Your train went north, mine
Towards York across the Pennines.
Never before had the hills
Seemed so green; in every valley
The sheltered mills shone
Bright with illusory gold.

Journey

It was new to see the dark. All the shops
had lights; in front of each
flat gardens of light lay on the pavement.
The tram swung along.

There is no sound in this memory,
no clank of tram, though the tram sways.
No talk. What kind of words would she be saying?
Her mouth moves around words. Her body
flings and fidgets, restless
with the excitement
of darkness and yellow light.
A varnished bench
follows the rounded
panels and windows
of the tram's deck.
She kneels on the seat, stares
out of the curve of glass
downward and backward
along thin steely tracks.

I can see her father now; can nearly see him.
He seems a calm young man,
overcoated, blond and broad.
He is her steadiness.
She is not old enough to wonder,
to need a reason for the outing.
She falls asleep against his tweed.

She is in his arms. They enter
the passage of the narrow house.
The slender hands of maiden great-aunts
flutter in welcome. She sways
between the soft brownness of their skirts.

In the Victorian dimness
flat white towels on a rail,
high soft bed that is not hers,
her father hurrying away.

Semi-detached

The tap marked hot in the bathroom
Was dry; for a bowlful
Of hot water, kettles must be boiled,
Carried upstairs. Easier,
The morning chores done,
For my mother to fill an enamel
Basin, wash herself at the kitchen table.

She would screw tight
Her marmalade hair, take off
Her glasses and blouse, stand
In her shiny slip. The heat
Flushed her fair skin,
Almost raised wheals
On her neck. Her eyes seemed wary;
An angry score of red linked them
Across the bridge of her nose.
Pearly water dripped
From her elbows, ran down
Between her breasts. I was glad
When a hasty towelling and a clean blouse
Brought her back to me unchanged.

Emma

I saw my mother cry for the first time
When Emma died;
She sat on my bed weeping.
Dead. What was dead?
A no more; too much to undertand.

Lucky to have had an Emma,
To have loved her, every inch
Of her five feet tall,
Known every wrinkle, all
The mumbles of her jaw,
White hair of head and chin,
The rolling walk
Her short leg gave her.

She would carry things
In a slung pocket between petticoats
(She wore five, black satteen,
To keep out cold and heat
Both in due season).

Undressing for bed we would perform
And pirouette for her and she would sing
Old songs about Jim Crow for lullaby
And nod herself to sleep.

She'd take all day to clean the stair-rods,
Two hours to wash the dishes,
Hated to go home, staying long after dark.

A pensioner, she came daily
For a little wage, her meals,
A lot of life. Our semi was her palace
We her princes. When my mother flagged
Or seemed inadequate she'd say,
'There's cart horses, m'm, and there's carriage horses;
They're not meant to be the same.'
Who would not weep to lose
So staunch a comforter?

Remembering Menuhin

On my first day away from home
we walked in the park. The bare grey path
seemed to stretch endlessly. Slight trees
semaphored in a March wind that searched
my skirt with an icy tongue, found flesh
above stocking-tops.

My aunt lived upstairs – the upper floor
of a semi in Willesden Green. In the small
room where I slept the bed fitted tight
against three of its walls, a close
safe place, but I missed my mother.

Each hour was a slab of boredom.
Except one day as we ate roast lamb
and then rice pudding, and then drank tea
a violin played – all that time –
from the wireless. 'Imagine!' said my aunt,
'Only a boy, playing like that!'

And every morning there were the ten minutes
when we watched from our window,
across a convent wall. The older nuns
walked briskly, marching pairs;
the young ones within their long black skirts
dodged and pursued each other, playing tag.
They ran about on the grass between the paths
of the closed garden, almost dancing
though no music could be heard.

That was Shell

A slow Ceres,
Country girl in town;
In derision they gave her a nickname,
Shell.

She lived near Oxford Street.
In a mean wind
We walked there together.
She wore a cloak.
Her mottled bare legs made me question
Whether it was for warmth or for convention
I darned my stockings nightly.

Suburban, family-bounded, I
Observed and began to envy
The uncommitted traffic of shared rooms,
The pastless furniture.
Envied the lack of love?
That too.
Wind-blown, searching for new ways
I hovered unfledged on the edge of talk
And dared not plunge.

Shell. She
Gave me tea and brown toast.
My mother had never dreamed
Of bread cut thick
Or brown bread toasted.
I felt the first chafe of my carapace.
A chink opened in it,
Fine as hair.

Daphne Morse

I'd not thought of her for twenty years
except from time to time, coming across
the old snap of us at Scarborough,
its yellowed monochrome
showing us both laughing on the beach,
my springing red hair printed as dark
as her lustrous black.

Daphne Morse. We were always laughing together,
seeing facades as faces, windows as eyes,
sharing jokes and confidences.
And how we admired each other! And sought
adventure, making aimless journeys,
lodging in attics and cottages, discovering
high moors in the short summer.

It was so long ago, her death,
the scar of it healed, faded;
and yet today unreasonably, unprompted,
I've grieved with a clear bitterness
for her, shortlived
and lovely Daphne Morse.
Thought how her cheeks bloomed
and her throat was smooth
and so were mine, bloomy, smooth.

The looking-glass
is half my present grief.

Casualties

There was dust on her sideboard
and she had a lodger, lugubrious man
who carried tea to her in bed.
We were taught to think her frivolous

or worse. Instead of dusting she'd sit
in the garden and read Mary Webb
while the lodger pottered, planted.
He was less than consort to her queen,

she made that clear, no consolation
for the young husband, foundered
in anonymous mud at Passchendaele,
two weeks out of England and newly-wed.

The baby, grief's frail doll,
had died on a pillow in her arms.
Of small concern thereafter how thick
the dust, who brings the morning tea.

Mother

Too late. I understand
why she wrote all those letters,
talked interminably of distant friends.
I seemed not to be needed
except as a sounding-board
when I visited.

The word's there: visited.
I should have stayed closer,
brought another kind of conversation,
made her speak directly.

She hung words between us
like gauze across a stage.
I could see only half the action;
my side of the truth.

I never saw her wounds;
she bandaged to conceal them.
Maybe in the dark
they healed a little,
and so did mine as I grew freer
of her conventions.

Not free enough. Never asking
or answering real questions
we would sit like husks
rustling in the room together.

Too late. I can't say to her
I know.
I know now she was lonely
in that muffling web, speaking
only of what seemed to be.

Doorsteps

Cutting bread brings her hands back to me –
the left, with its thick wedding ring,
steadying the loaf. Small plump hands
before age shirred and speckled them.

She would slice not downwards but across
with an unserrated ivory-handled carving knife
bought from a shop in the Edgware Road,
an Aladdin's cave of cast-offs from good houses –
earls and countesses were hinted at.

She used it to pare to an elegant thinness.
First she smoothed already-softened butter
on the upturned face of the loaf. Always white,
Coburg shape. Finely rimmed with crust the soft
halfmoon half-slices came to the tea table
herringboned across a doylied plate.

I saw away at stoneground wholemeal.
Each slice falling forward into the crumbs,
to be spread with butter's counterfeit
is as thick as three of hers. Doorsteps,
she'd have called them. And those were white
in our street, rubbed with hearthstone
so that they glared in the sun
like new-dried tennis shoes.

Window

Sometimes, everyone in bed,
she would need to flit across
the lit landing in the night,
go down a few stairs
to the lavatory, her face
blank with sleep, hair a dulled
fuzzed halo, a little barefoot figure
hurrying in a nightdress.
The long window that in daylight
showed apple leaves and sky
faced her, a black mirror.
There a lonely ghost child
stepped towards her
turned, when she turned,
as if to descend the stair
and then was left behind,
contained where the frame ended,
the wall's solidity began.

Returning, her cold soles
quick on the hard floor, she knew
though she did not risk a look,
that at the head of the stairs
the other child would have come again,
only to retreat, to run
into the depth behind the glass.
Fear fingering its spine,
nightdress folds flowing back,
it would be running
away along phantom floorboards
to where treetops were drowned
in the brimming dark
of the looking-glass garden.

Kestrel

He lay on his breast against the house wall
The brass rings of his eyes still polished.
He must have arrowed full-tilt
Into the first floor window-glass
Making just one mistake
About space.

Handsomely banded sweeping wings,
Half-folded, hunched his shoulders
Like the pinions of a tabby angel.
His face narrowed wisely
To the small beak like a single horn
Delicately designed to hinge apart
And rend flesh.

After a week he's nothing.
Only his hard legs are fierce,
Stretching out talons
Hollow, flexible, smooth,
The colour of polished lava.
He lies on his back now, wings fallen apart,
Head like a wet pebble,
Ribcage small as a child's fist
Arching under a drenched grey vest.
His underfeathers flattened and swirled by rain
Look like a map
Of the world's winds.

Pastoral

(T.S. Cooper, R.A., 1803-1902)

I can see a man might want
Like Cooper, to paint cows
By rivers, under trees,
Lying or standing, slow, gregarious,
Unconscious that each leisured
Bite they take feeds us.

But that's no thought of Cooper's.
He just liked their shapes
And colours in the meadows
(As who does not?).
He liked their humid eyes, their breath
Steamy with perished flowers,
Their swelling sides
And shopping-basket udders
And deliberate feet
Treading housewifely home.

And so he painted them,
Cow after cow after cow.

A.I. Bulls

West of Totnes I look out for them,
Flashed in the frame of the train window,
An unmatched ponderous assembly
Chained, branded with resignation,
Aligned like harboured boats.

In farmyards I had been always
Timid, wisely skirting away
From baffled thud and roar, the huge-fleshed
Contumaceous danger contained
Behind scarred wood, secure latch,
But these stand passive as virgin uncles
Enduring the circumstance that distances them
From frenzy and the season's odours.
In their shared field they seem as patient
As a group of chairbound aged
Waiting for teatime.

Humanly I regret for them
Their passionless stance,
The husbanding of their seed, the routine
Relief of its taking, its sowing
Without touch of kind to kind.
I would wish them to be bullgods
But they are semen-batteries,
Bestowers of calculated excellence.
Making patterns for dynasties
They earn survival, maleness.

In the whole long landscape of the journey
Are seen no others like these;
Only the young unsexed herds
Wheeling flank to flank in illusory freedom
Or staring amazed among tides of buttercups.

Harvest

They were summers full of sunshine. In the fields
We would creep into the stooks of tilted sheaves,
Crouching with scratched legs
Among the sharp-cut stubble. Tight to dry earth
Too low for blades to catch grew speedwell
Blue as cornflower, pimpernel
Red as poppy.

From two-tined shining forks, long handles worn
To patina by hard palms, the sheaves flew high
Onto carts lead-red and blue-sky painted.
The wheels rolled heavy-hubbed and iron-rimmed
Weightily field to stack and lighter back again
Between straw-littered hedges dull with dust.

As the day drooped to evening we'd ride the wide backs
Of Boxer or Diamond to the farmyard. Freed from shafts,
Greasy black straps swinging, they could wade
Into the pond, drink, bend their great necks.
It was the men's joke not to lift us down
But thwack the chestnut rumps, send us to balance
Above the surface smeared with sap-green weed.

They teased us, town children, made us brave;
And I remember them, the faces, names, speech,
Working clothes and movements of those men,
The perks they carried home; skimmed milk in cans,
Field cabbages in sacks, soft rabbits
Swinging head-down from loops of twine, to feed
Long families of uncombed dusty children
Who stood at laneside gates,
Watched us without a smile.

Pressed Man

None of them's modest, nor maidens,
And if they were, what good to us?
Draggle-dressed, gap-toothed, wild,
But they're what we need.
They weather such storms, these old tarts,
Without ever leaving harbour; like gales
We bear them down flat on the planks.
The officers go ashore
(As we pressed men cannot) and I wager
Are soon out of their sleek breeks
Working for once as willingly as we
And at the same task, but snug
And private in a wide bed.

Time was I slept in a bed; not with a wench though.
I was twelve years old, but tall, could labour
Like a man, plough like a man, the brown rump
Of the mare steady before me, her tail like tresses,
The share biting the earth. A good way to live,
I remember the white seabirds
Crowding in from the storm to follow me.
They would fly twenty leagues to cheat
The plovers of a few poor worms.

When the pressgang came I was working the long field,
Saw the man waiting toward the furrow's end.
Would have left all, plough, horse, and run from him
But there were others beside and behind me.

In my mind old Poll still stands in the cold field
As doubtless she did that day until nightfall.
I think my father would have wept for loss of me,
Loosing the harness, leading the mare home.

Harbour is what seabirds mean now
And a whore – but no foot
On land. They've made me a sailor.
I'll never have wife or roof
And, dead, shall go over the side.
The sea's belly is full of us pressed men.

Threshold

My mother, saying only
This is for when your time comes,
gave me a stick of wood, scarred
by the marks of teeth.

She made no explanation
but touched me at breast and waist.
I did not tell her that my moon-blood
had ceased to flow; nor did I ask

the wise woman when my belly waxed
why that should be, though I feared
the movements within, and my steps
grew slow with the weight I bore.

When the angry rippling began to surge
through and through my flesh the women
led me to the valley that was no man's.
Pitiless tides possessed me.

The stubborn wood that my mother's teeth
had bruised was in my mouth.
I strove against it, biting hard,
and the grain held.

Still I did not know for how long
the pain might last, how fierce its peak
nor its purpose. Clasping the women's hands,
groaning against the clenched wood,

I thrust as if to cast out death. But life
slid from me onto the spread rushes,
a new mouth cried out. The wooden talisman
is my trust for this child when she grows.

And she shall have more:
my careful words against fear.

Guest Room

There is no mirror in the room.

First morning I present myself
as if in an unrehearsed mask
and am recognised.

Each day on I further
lose knowledge of my face, relearn
body shapes; my public limbs, the curve
of my pale private belly.

I become simpler, less diffuse.
Reflections perhaps steal concentration
as, it is said, the camera
robs, takes soul to make images.

Fifth day at breakfast I remember
I've not combed my hair. Who
sees me if a mirror does not?

Rings

This morning's letter is a hungry one.
His wife will be waking as I read.
I can't wait – he writes – Longing to . . .
longing to . . .
But in truth he can take
or leave me, and I him.

I have four old rings.
One, topaz, a clustered
flower set in silver; another
two hands clasped masking
a beaten silver heart;
a third fine gold set with jet
inscribed 1822, in memory . . .
last, a farthing-sized amethyst,
flat-cut, clawed in gold,
incised with the image of a quill
and the mirror-imaged words
The Tongue of the Absent.

To him I write nothing.
My answer will be without words
a selfish taking and giving,
daily crinoline yawning on the stair,
public petticoats falling one by one.

Love Lyrics

He'd take it from the stiff
black leather box where it lived
safe on a high shelf. Razor;
dangerous elegant instrument,
his personal property and privilege.
It flashed as he stropped
skimming the dark supple strap.
We heard the soft thumping rhythm,
and the song. Tosti's Farewell.
You that I worshipped so.

We'd loll in the bathroom doorway
while he lathered up, cut skilful
flat swathes through the marshmallow soap.
Still he sang, that young man who since
has had no choice but to grow old
and die. *Less than the dust*, he sang,
Beneath thy chariot wheels.

Brushing his red-gold hair he'd lean
towards the mirror and sing con espressione
Pale hands I loved beside the Shalimar.
We glimpsed worlds to come,
our own true loves.

I had not then heard, whispered
between the rows of damp school coats,
the facts of sex; had much more to learn.
His songs had not been for my mother alone,
a duplicity the years disclosed.
There was no more singing, no bright
old-fashioned blade. He took to the tame
safety razor, closed the bathroom door.

The Half Mile

I was twelve when I swam the half-mile,
up and down the tide-fed cold concrete
pool, with a slow steady sidestroke.
My father counted the lengths,
at first from the deep-end board
and then, as I moved more laboriously,
pacing alongside, urging me on.

The race was only against myself
and distance. The grainy salt water,
though not translucent like the chlorinated
blue lidos of town, buoyed me helpfully,
lapped softly against the bath's grey sides
variegated with embedded hardcore pebbles.
I swam from goal to alternate goal; he counted.

When he called enough I scrambled
over the sharp shutter-cast lip,
shuddered into a dry towel, drank
the words of praise. The planks
of the changing-room walls
were warm to touch. It had seemed to be
a great deal of swimming; still does.

Iced Coffee

They never afforded close carpeting,
only practical squares of brown
leafpatterned Axminster, never
a washing-machine or a fridge.
It was always either one thing
or another, a balancing of choices.

One winter Sunday afternoon
my father sprang up suddenly
from the quiet of his chair, tugged
at his trouser pocket
and flung onto the hearthrug
a clattering handful of loose change
crying, 'That's what I am, a penny man!'
He longed for flamboyance –
a dashing Edwardian role,
tossing careless sovereigns.

Retirement freed him from the suburbs.
The dark-beamed rose-hung house
lent him at last the aura
of a leisured man of means.
He accepted village chairmanships,
kept geese and a bulldog, trundled
to Taunton in his old Humber, buying
buckets and fertilisers; would harvest
armfuls of vegetables, dump them
on the kitchen table, leave trails
of boot-mud on the terracotta shine –
all with an air of release, and pride
in everything from the mended thatch
to the new fridge against the larder wall.

On my first visit he settled me
in a garden chair, brought tall glasses.
His blue-eyed smile of triumph belied
his Noel Coward pose.
'Iced coffee?' he offered, casually.

The Lepidopterist

The narrow room was lined with cabinets
of pale polished wood, many drawers
each shallow as a frying pan.
One at a time he pulled them forward,
exhibited the impeccably tidy corpses within –
chorus-lines of identical cream-soft virgins
and companies of camp-followers gaudy
in tortoiseshell, crimson; all noncombatants.
Some, he said, were rare.
And every one was perfect.

Hundreds. He went on showing, describing them,
making no mistakes for each was mounted
as he remembered from the years when
with clear sight he'd made
this mortuary of wings.

Blind now, he dared no longer
bring his fingers near to touch, enjoy.
Their frailty defeated him. He'd not know
whether they lay firm like pharaohs
or sank against their white cards
to spooned dust, escaping him, dead things
that on the wing had not escaped his net,
his slumbrous bottle, his sharp pin.

Spencer Park

A saffron autumn, hardly any red
Or russet, or brown yet;
Leaves bleached in random patterns
Lighten daily to melon-ripeness,
Soft as sleepy pears.

Rising from waves of scumbled
Darkly green gorse, dormant,
Sparsely sparked with bloom,
A copse of silver birches
Tosses up fountains of small yellow flames,
Celebrates the ending
Of the late Indian summer.

At evening under lanterns strung from boughs
We eat and drink and stand wet-soled
In grass unnaturally emerald.
Candle flames trapped in jars
Dwindle along paths.
Children wheel about in coltish herds
Full of night-freedom, the excitement
Of flame-ferns curling,
Red sparks tracer-shooting
Through the slow waltz of the climbing smoke.

Fireworks, crackling torrents of white and coloured light,
Will not live so gentle in the mind
As the warm bonfire cavern scooped out of the dark
Or as the slow daylight burning
Of the birch trees' living leaves.

In Memoriam

Mae West is dead, the most
Danny la Rue of all female
Female impersonators, a lady
Of provocative phrases, her words
A waving flag on the crest
Of a mountain of implication.

Queen of saloon girls,
Bigtime siren and always
Her own mistress, she swanned
Through the envious secret dreams
Of wives, her prowed bosom
Heavy with earned jewels.

Dying in bed, in a female world,
She was blanket-bathed and fed
By nurses, young, and I dare say
Not a virgin amongst them,
So unsequined now is sex, no longer
A naughty mystery and nothing to do
With talk of drifted snow.
Nowadays
We peel our own grapes.

Mater Regina

Age, sudden as frost
has embroidered upon me
the patterns of its contagion;
my stiff tread
declares it like bells.
Not for me now, nor again,
the answering flesh
the warm lips
of a young man.

I watch them, their muscled arms,
the vigour of their thighs.
They laugh from the deep ease
of their round throats
and are inaccessible to me
as the newborn are
to the long-dead.

I, Jocasta, shall not sleep again.
My bed has been my snare. The rope,
plain friend, waits undisguised
to swing me out of life, away
from my twice-loved son,
the raped face of his grief,
the fountains of red tears
that are my blood.

Home is the Hunter

She's watched for his return
at each day's evening, his briefcase
stuffed as if with deermeat,
umbrella a spent spear.
Forty years of triumphal entrances,
attentive welcomings, end in this
gift-loaded euphoric homecoming.
Something near to fear

stirs in her. The house
has been hers throughout the core
of every day, close shelter
for her busy morning hours,
her re-creative afternoons.
Now it opens its traitor door,
switches allegiance to his clamour,
his masterfulness, his more

insistent needs. How long had she
dug, hoed and planted the suburban
flower-patch, made it colourful
and fragrant for his weekend
leisure? Now he comes in with the air
of a pioneer, as if her patient garden
were wilderness for his first
cultivation; and she'll pretend

(habits are hard to break) when called on
to admire, that everything he grows
is magical, as if no million years
but he alone made this summer's rose.

Near Neighbours

In this house the turnover of crockery
has been as perceptible over the years
as the rotation of crops in a familiar field.
Blue-banded cups and saucers, ethnic
brown beakers that wore rough at the lip,
then supermarket mugs, variously decorated –
mock-Victorian advertisements for corsets
or sewing machines rubbing sides with clusters
of crudely-bright fruit, wide red poppies,
or butterflies or a circle of Valentine hearts
and LOVE IS . . . . . .

The china in the other house never changes.
The family drinks from shapely cups,
eats from flute-edged plates until flower
and leaf emerge. A meal over, the dresser
bears again on every hook and shelf, blooms
carefully lustrous from suds and teatowel.
Throughout a marriage (and never an interloper
from Lawley's or the Co-op given houseroom)
the subtle pinks and greens have shone
beneath a pale glaze, uniform and uncrazed.
Each cloned rose could be last month's
replacement or a survivor from the first
purchase still unscathed.

I visit the other house, but am always glad
to be back home, amongst ephemera.
A teabag steeps in the stained cylinder
of my currently-favoured porcelain mug
printed with apples whole and halved.
I stir to tease out strength, spoon up
the sodden bag, add milk. Drinking,
listening to silence, I wonder
if my neighbours' children will be gardeners,
grow standard roses along straight paths;
wonder what harm or good will have stemmed
from my haphazard table, the brown clay,
the garish unvalued poppies.

Stanley Spencer: Resurrection at Port Glasgow

As friendly a lot of people
as one could wish to meet.
They climb hopefully
from their incarceration,
well-nourished, in the pink,
their clothes countrified
but miraculously recent in style
and free from any trace of soil.

Their limbs are a bit stiff
but that will soon wear off.
They're cheerful, not a bit surprised
that the promised amnesty has really
come about. See how they help each other
and are not afraid. Though what next?

My guess is that soon, limbered up,
they'll all stroll, gossiping
as if to make up for lost time
through the open gate to the vicarage
for cups of tea and some of Mrs God's
special light sponge cakes
and scones; hot, buttery. Mmmm . . . .

Turkish Village

No paths.
Ledges of ranged rocks
Like the shone foreheads of old skulls
Lead painfully upward.
Carobs clenching the rust-dry soil
Are heavy with beans.
Chicks chirp, and cicadas.
The people are quiet in the heat,
Watching behind walls
Where geraniums bubble red
Out of old oilcans.
The land
Burns our shod feet.

By the jetty there is chai.

Welcome and goodbye
Are the flash of a gold tooth.

Leaving the Party

At two o'clock, the last full moon of the year,
The night immaculate, starchy with frost,
I stood in the square of gold
Thrown with the noise of talk and music
Across the silent air
Onto the leaves of sleeping bushes.
I took in my hand
A finial bud of rhododendron
Closely bound in a brown tissue
Like cloth from the Egyptian dead,
Like the stained graveclothes
Of all who hoped to live again
Listening to the words
Of Isis or Jesus.

Come Away

His name
filled my scream
I ran barefoot down the stairs
fast as the childhood dream

when lions follow;
up again I ran,
the stairs a current of air
blew me like thistledown.

I laid my palm on his calf
and it was warm and muscled
and like life.

Come away said the kind doctor.
I left the body there
lying straight, our wide bed
a single bier.

All night I watched
tree branches scratch the sky,
printed another window-frame
for ever on my eye.

When I came home in the morning
all the warmth had gone.
I touched his useless hand.
Where his eyes had shone
behind half-lifted lids were grown
cataracts of stone.

When You Died

1.

When you died
I went through the rain
Carrying my nightmare
To register the death.

A well-groomed healthy gentleman
Safe within his office
Said – Are you the widow?

Couldn't he have said
Were you his wife?

2.

After the first shock
I found I was
Solidly set in my flesh.
I was an upright central pillar,
The soft flesh melted round me.
My eyes melted
Spilling the inexhaustible essence of sorrow.
The soft flesh of the body
Melted onto chairs and into beds
Dragging its emptiness and pain.

I lodged inside holding myself upright,
Warding off the dreadful deliquescence.

3.

November.
Stooping under muslins
Of grey rain I fingered
Through ribbons of wet grass,
Traced stiff stems down to the wormy earth
And one by one snapped off
The pale surviving flowers; they would ride
With him, lie on the polished plank
Above his breast.

People said – Why do you not
Follow the coffin?
Why do you not
Have any funeral words spoken?
Why not
Send flowers from a shop?

4.

When you died
They burnt you.
They brought home to me
A vase of thin metal;
Inside, a plastic bag
Crammed, full of gritty pieces.
Ground bones, not silky ash.

Where shall I put this substance?
Shall I scatter it
With customary thoughts
Of nature's mystical balance
Among the roses?

Shall I disperse it into the winds
That blow across Cambeake Cliff
Or drop it onto places where you
Lived, worked, were happy?

Finally shall I perhaps keep it
Which after all was you
Quietly on a shelf
And when I follow
My old grit can lie
No matter where with yours
Slowly sinking into the earth together.

5.

When you died
I did not for the moment
Think about myself;
I grieved deeply and purely for your loss,
That you had lost your life.
I grieved bitterly for your mind destroyed,
Your courage thrown away,
Your senses aborted under the amazing skin
No one would ever touch again.

I grieve still
That we'd have grown
Even more deeply close and old together
And now shall not.

Two Years

When you died
All the doors banged shut.

After two years, inch by inch,
They creep open.
Now I can relish
Small encounters,
Encourage
Small flares of desire;
Begin to believe as you did
Things come right.
I tell myself that you
Escaped the slow declension to old age
Leaving me to indulge
This wintry flowering.

But I know
It's not like that at all.

Four Years

The smell of him went soon
From all his shirts.
I sent them for jumble,
And the sweaters and suits.
The shoes
Held more of him; he was printed
Into his shoes. I did not burn
Or throw or give them away.
Time has denatured them now.

Nothing left.
There will never be
A hair of his in a comb.
But I want to believe
That in the shifting housedust
Minute presences still drift:
An eyelash,
A hard crescent cut from a fingernail,
That sometimes
Between the folds of a curtain
Or the covers of a book
I touch
A flake of his skin.

View from the Train

St Mary Reddecliffe's spire; beneath it
we'd talked of Chatterton, ill-fated clever boy,
and the romantic deathbed painting in the Tate.
No thought then of real death, the capricious
equaliser, unequally removing.

My brown boy, my soft-hearted
hard-willed man, you also were not meant
to grow weak-thighed, to totter and fumble.
I have learned this, watching old men
slow walking, nodding as they talk
and smile purple-lipped at their deaf
wrinkled wives. Well, we shall not
see each other so degraded,
you unknowing now, me travelling on.

Five Years

These are not desired or indulged tears;
acid, insistent, they have harassed my eyelids
all day, and now in the room where he died
they fall like leaves falling
without volition or noise.

Recall after recall comes, single moments
free from the motives, the confusions
of circumstance that forced us
to waste ourselves and our
time; they pour through my memory,
still do not make a pattern.

The summit of grief is passed. How
do I learn to live with the helpless rage,
begin to accept death's barren truth?
Hand in hand go disbelief and the fear
of my own moment to come, rankling
like the fear of the first
act of love
the first parturition.

That Winter

He made night journeys; three hundred miles, then
a day's work and a second night's haul home
in a governed lorry, never more than forty
miles an hour. It had to be nursed along,
that old green diesel, listened to. Uphill
needed particular skill, forbearance
from clutch and gearstick until momentum
slackened, revs fell to the crucial count.

Sometimes I'd ride with him. We could talk
only at road junctions and traffic lights,
so loudly the engine's boxed voice boomed
between us. We'd sit self-contained
and silent, watching the lit wedge of road
often sliced monotonously by the scything
windscreen wipers, all brilliances
multiplied and distorted in the rain.

The best nights were when the moon eased
our journey, burnishing the metal way,
revealing distance on either hand.
Buoyed in the lightened sky
she would seem to float alongside
or to lead or follow as the road turned
across rivers, traced the roots of hills,
made a wide circle to gain the motorway.

Worst were the nights of ice
when fog billowed against the cold glass
thickening the air with droplets that baffled
our yellow light, obscured the verges
behind a shivering gauze. Gloved, scarfed,
only our eyes hot with strain, we searched
our way through barriers of vapour that dawn
would blanch but not dispel. All winter

I watched his cheeks grow gaunt, the flesh
fall from his bones, while he denied exhaustion.
I remember how on those journeys he comforted me,
a hand on my knee, still gazing ahead, driving
inexorably on. At his side I was lost
in sleepless dreams, shadowy avenues where great trees
frowned like thunderheads from the cold sky
and seemed to follow like the moon, but dark.

Coronary

He could have died driving
on a motorway and dragged
another twelve surprised souls
in his wake; or in a supermarket

so that the customers
went home disturbed, not hungry
for their dinners. He could
have halted a fast train,

have fallen forward as it sliced
through the station. Businessmen
would have been late for appointments
and children on the platform

would never have forgotten
in some part of their minds
the fear that froze the sunshine.
But, giving no hurt

to any stranger, he climbed
the stair to our own room,
his will not quite enough
to bring him to the bed.

Coming to Terms

In nearly thirty years he would not say
he loved me. At first I found it hard
having to believe without the words
my upbringing had led me to expect

that he did indeed desire
and need me enough to have gladly
abandoned all others for my sake.
In vulnerable moments I might dare

rashly to ask the forbidden question;
he was adamant, allowing me only
the explanation that, for him,
the word had become debased,

currency of cheap fiction designed
to daze the half-literate. No use
evoking Donne and Shakespeare;
other times, other values.

Growing in love for him, perforce unspoken,
I came to see his reticence as trust,
as tribute to my strength.
The approach of death also

we faced silently, on his terms.
You might say now I have liberty of speech.
Through unshared rooms year after year
I spin words. At first they all

seemed precious, each of intrinsic value.
Now I see they are threads that anyone
may weave; worth's in fine cloth,
a warm coat sewn to fit.

The Gate

A gull flew low across the garden
his spread sails white as washing
against blue sky on a good drying day

and I was back in Mevagissey, the wings
and cries, and the houses so close
that clothes are pegged high,

strung out from upper windows
on line and pulley to catch the air.
One day, standing for a moment

at the kitchen door I caught sight
of something half submerged moving along
the channel that ran to the harbour

through the backyards of that street.
It was some thing of yours lost days before
into the stream at the head of the valley

delivered home by water
with such nicety of coincidence.
What it was escapes me now.

Was it orange coloured, a size
to fit the palm? What weight and shape?
The searching has opened another closed gate.

There you are, not a hair lost; and the man
who was our child is flaxen again, naked,
laughing down from a forbidden rock.

The beach was yellow then before
the nightstorm that drew the sand away
dispersed its grains under the sea.

I should be sorry if the dead

I should be sorry if the dead indeed
Clustered about us, eager to communicate
Through the fickle mouths of mediums
In hired halls and dusty meeting-rooms.
Surely they have better choices?

It is sad to think of some watershed
Of spirits attendant on our love or hate,
Committed to our small tediums
And tied to our lives until perhaps new wombs
Case them in substance, flesh out their voices.

And must they wait about till all
The intimates of a life die too, before they end
Their spirit vigilance in case a call
Comes from a grandchild or a friend?

I should be sorry if the dead lived on
With neither rest nor heaven of their own.

Skin

It was sheer silk once, silk
from toe to brow; is as fine now
only in the smooth hollow
between collarbone and breast.
Tucked into my shrugged shoulder
my cheek browses
for the linger of perfection.

Ah, Helen! Were you lifted flawless
to the stars, or did you live on,
vulnerable to time, answered
by mirrors? Did truth gaze back
from some unruffled pool, or bathing
as became your state in marble's
luxurious lap, did you see
with sad acknowledgement
the crêpe-de-chine of hands
and forearms, the change from smooth
to slack no ointment could reverse?

And seeing, did you fear
there might be no more love?

Chocolate Cake

In the Italian café at Earls Court
we asked for coffee but the minimum fee –
late night and Sunday – meant we also got
slices of chocolate cake. We ate and talked
and were the last to leave. We didn't see
the coffee-maker wiping clean his urn,
sat on dry-islanded, a film of shine
veneered around us where the mop had slopped
(all chairs but ours had been conveniently
uplifted onto tables); nor had we
heard these manoeuvres. Midnight streets; we walked
as if to a shared bed. But there it stopped.
I'd learned too much of him to wantonly
beggar his conscience. Nothing's really free.

Rime on Coal

The early fast train paused (signals
malfunctioning they said), just time
to notice a tarred hut white-crystalled;
an iron marker on a trackside pole –
75 ciphered in frost-furred sable; and below,
a coalyard, bays heaped with black fruit sized
and graded, the difference outlined in rime.

Then, without fuss – no blustering
hardbreathing start, no steam coughed
white on the blue air – our yellow engine
nosed again into the cold, smoothly
gathered speed. Limousine travelling.
Crossword puzzlers, coffee drinkers, children
finishing out their sleep, felt no jolt.
White landscapes slid by. I closed my eyes,
sank into a railway daydream.

Huge presences they were, with huffs and puffs
and sudden screaming whistles.
My father once, blind to my clinging terror,
carried me down the acrid platform's length,
lifted me to see the engine-driver leaning
oilsmeared from the high footplate
and the monstrous impatient locomotive's
tight heart of fire.

They had the power of mistresses, those old engines,
hankered after for their odours, their voices,
their panting appetites. Satisfied, they repaid
with all their might, fast beauties. Even now
in pensioned age they exact homage. Admirers
gather to polish and preserve them,
and speak with reverence their brazen names.

Over the Ocean

She wrote in an airletter how
every cavity of his chest invaded,
tubed, with not even the relief
of swallowing his saliva, he'd joked
about his poor life expectancy.

There were no words of grief,
as if she'd not dared to capitulate.
He hadn't even smoked –
she might have felt bitter about that,
but rather she seemed disconsolate
that he'd died far from old friends
and before time, all his talents,
his marvellous flair for life,
leaching away long hopeless months
in a hospital bed.

She'd sent no letters in the eight months
of his dying; and now these bare unmourning
lines. Yet, suffusing the plain sentences,
her hurt blooms like a bruise.
He'd closed her out from death, worn humour
like a victor's wreath, disguised his fear,
asked nothing from her, would not bare
his dying thoughts to her, or share
any weakness, not a tear.

Passing Marks Tey

I used to see the old men sunning themselves,
a village parliament by the south side of a barn.
Grass clumped by the wall; between the uprights
of the bench the earth was bootworn, brown.

I could almost smell the ashy bowls of the pipes
they sucked, their musty hats, as we passed through
towards deeper country where men in the fields
straightened their backs when motorcars went by.

We travelled into Suffolk, slowed by punctures
and running-board picnics. My father's bargain tourer
had a toolbox, a starting handle, a leather hood.
Such cars belong to the rich now, or to museums.

When I drove through Essex I passed Marks Tey
on a fast road; saw no bench, no new old men.
I thought of them indoors watching faces that can't listen
and plays about peace and war impeccably researched.

No Smoking
(for Jack Watson)

Boarding innumerable trains over the years
I've chosen always to sit by the ring
of red on the glass; and always my mind
repeats the litany: No Smoking – Nosmo King.

It was long ago, a summer in the thirties.
The pool was open-air, heated, brand new,
won from the tract of common land across
the road from school. We'd watched it grow,

a larger and larger hole, had searched
along the strata of its clay walls
for fossils, walking where water would soon lie.
Its space had the vastness of cathedrals,

railway termini, a sunken hollowness
that should have echoed, multiplied,
the high notes of our voices, but instead
each vertical drank sound into its dank side.

Slowly, concurrently, grew avenues
of cubicles and lockers; and at last the bright
blueness, clear to its ripple-chopped lane-lines.
There were high diving-boards, marble-white

fountains, green terraced lawns.
They found old Liz just hours before
the ceremony, floating in her rags; dead
in sorrow or in protest. It was more

than accident. On this land she'd built her rough
shelters of rubbish; we'd held her in mock fear,
poor broken-booted crone. How could she have lived on,
no gorse, or hawthorn left for structure?

So, whichever sleek swimmer made the ritual dive
to part the waveless water was not the first
comer, though more stylishly than she
he sprang, flew, was immersed

and rose towards the speech that heralded
our summer of lunchtime pleasures. We could just
hear well enough the afternoon school bell,
buttoned our shirts and blazers as we rushed

wet-haired to lessons. Those felicities
were shortlived; soon there was no more school,
but city jobs in banks and offices.
Only the weekends saw me at the pool

that year of dull weekdays, shining Saturdays,
when, although only once or twice,
(I almost silent, faced with such distinction)
you and I met and casually talked. Your eyes

were speedwell blue (I think), your limbs
of tempting shape, well-tanned, your hair
blond in the sunshine. Yes, I'm sure
it was plentiful and golden fair.

Hubert! – they nudged and said – You know!
Hubert and Nosmo King! Indeed I'd heard
your wireless voices; your father's rich
round tone echoes to me now, remembered

among much forgetting. But you're heard still
in drawing-rooms, convents, pubs. And seen. You've stood
in my bedroom clanking Roman arms
or sat, glowering, crusty, bringing a rude

lifestyle to my quiet table. The man
of presence who unknowing meets my eye
or that of thief or prince must still be he
who by the pool's balustrade lolled easily

in love, as we all were, with youth itself.
I too shone then with newness, in cheap blue
two-piece swimsuit, one of the shy
girls who'd steal a glance at you,

enjoying a small sideways brush with fame.
Such moments unpredictably I remember,
the April of my days. Where stands my calendar now?
And yours, too? Surely no later than September,

approaching Michaelmas. October's often fine,
November dull but seldom cold. We learn
in December life's last lessons. And then
will come a January that won't be our concern.

A Love Poem

There were two that mattered. Two.
Better than one only, or many small,
or none, the heart's desert.

Pain comes afterwards, when it's done,
can't ever be again, the full hunger
that nothing quite assuages,

the reaching that never quite touches,
the welling up never contained, brimmed
wastefully. Our bodies are less than enough

for the need to give. Eyes, speech, nakedness,
clasped hands, all die with flesh, but love
keeps growing like a genie, endlessly

pouring from the pinched neck of dark glass,
crying out – You did not ask enough.
There could have been more, more.